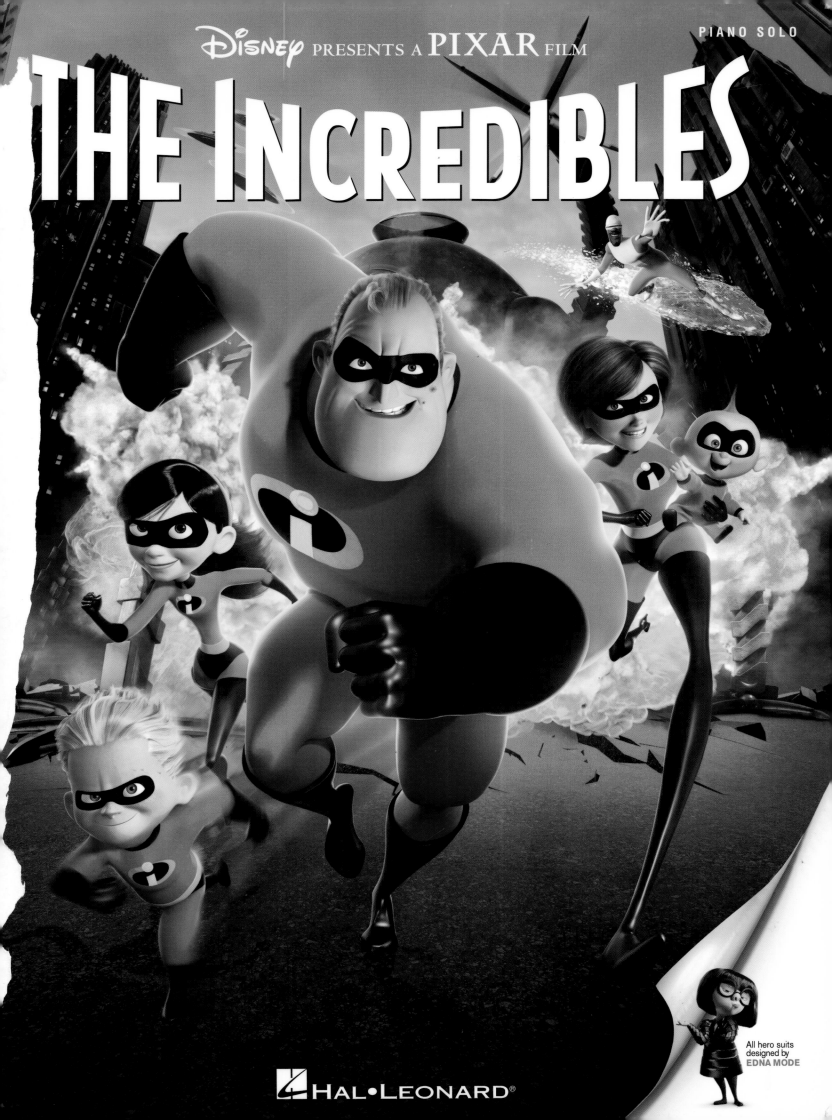

DISNEY PRESENTS A PIXAR FILM

# THE INCREDIBLES

ISBN 0-634-09516-1

In Australia Contact:
**Hal Leonard Australia Pty. Ltd.**
22 Taunton Drive  P.O. Box 5130
Cheltenham East, 3192  Victoria, Australia
Email:  ausadmin@halleonard.com

**Wonderland Music Company, Inc.**

DISTRIBUTED BY

HAL•LEONARD®
CORPORATION
7777 W. BLUEMOUND RD. P.O. BOX 13819 MILWAUKEE, WI 53213

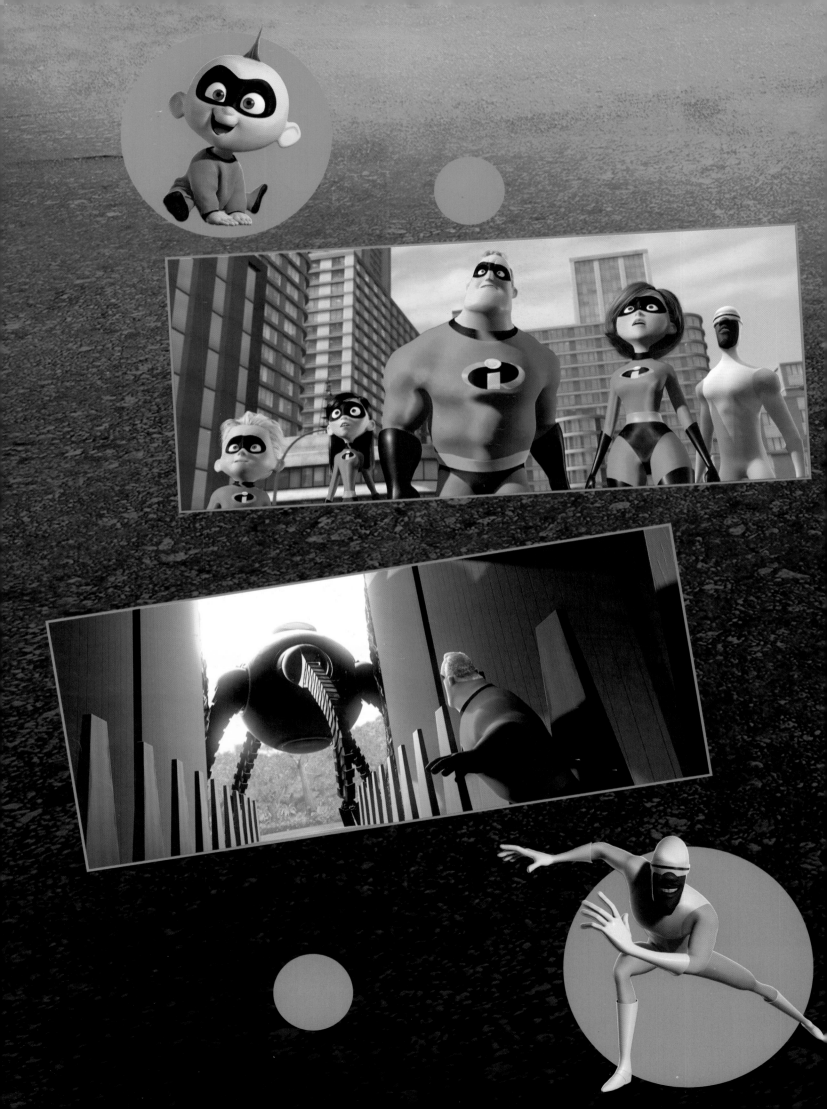

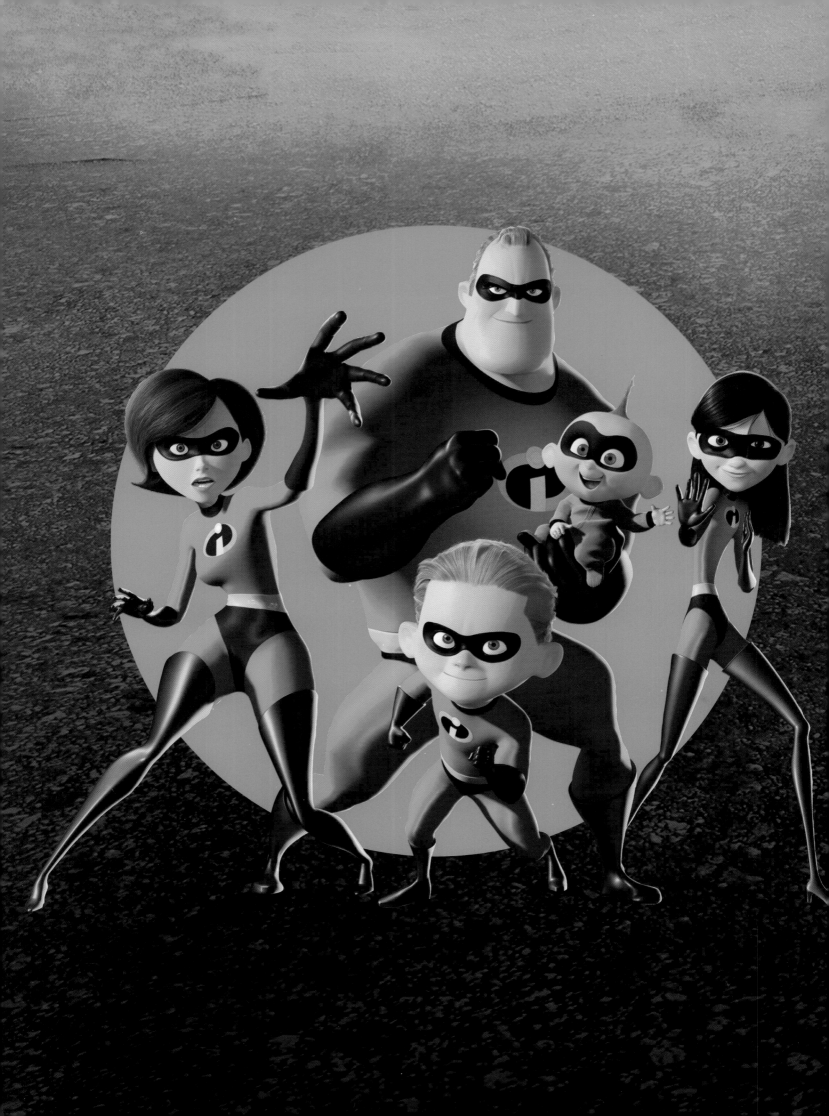

# THE GLORY DAYS

Music by MICHAEL GIACCHINO

8vb- - - - - - - - - - - - - - - - - - - - - - - - - - - - - - - - - - - - - - - - - - - - - - - - - - - - - - - - - - - - - - - - - - - - -

(8vb)- - - - - - - - - - - - - - - - - - - - - - - - - - - - - - - - - - - - - - - - - - - - - - - - -

# MR. HUPH WILL SEE YOU NOW

Music by MICHAEL GIACCHINO

Moderately, in 4

**Moderately fast**                    (♪ = ♪)

# LIFE'S INCREDIBLE AGAIN

Music by MICHAEL GIACCHINO

# OFF TO WORK

Music by MICHAEL GIACCHINO

Moderately

18

# MISSILE LOCK

Music by MICHAEL GIACCHINO

# LITHE OR DEATH

Music by MICHAEL GIACCHINO

**Moderately, expressively**

**Moderately fast, steadily**

# THE INCREDITS

Music by MICHAEL GIACCHINO

**Fast**

Sax solo ad lib.

Sax solo ends